All Rights Reserved © Easy Double Wedding Ring Quilt Pattern - 2nd Edition - Monna Ellithorpe 2004 - 2015

Disclaimer and Terms of Use: No information contained in this book should be considered as physical, health related, financial, tax, or legal advice. Your reliance upon information and content obtained by you at or through this publication is solely at your own risk. The author assumes no liability or responsibly for damage or injury to you, other persons, or property arising from any use of any product, information, idea, or instruction contained in the content provided to you through this book.

NOTE: Every effort has been made to ensure the accuracy of the templates when printed but because of the variations in printers on the market, the templates may not print accurately. Please refer to the measurements on the template page before cutting your fabric.

Table of Contents

DEDICATION..4

CUTTING INSTRUCTIONS:...........................6

SUPPLY LIST...7

STARTING YOUR QUILT…..........................9

CUTTING…..11

APPLYING STEAM-A-SEAM2....................14

WORKING WITH THE BACKGROUND......18

APPLYING CORNER OR CONNECTING SQUARES..22

JOINING YOUR QUILT BLOCKS................26

MAKING THE HALF BLOCKS FOR THE QUILT EDGE..28

TEMPLATES...33

About The Author - Monna Ellithorpe.............34

DEDICATION

This Book is Dedicated to my very dear friend Marie Eastwood.

A teacher affects eternity; he can never tell where his influence stops.

Henry B. Adams

In 1985 I worked with a lady who is now a very dear friend, Marie. She always worked on some kind of sewing project (i.e. sewing, quilting or crocheting) on our breaks or any minute of spare time that she had. I would sit and watch her and watching her quilt interested me more than anything.

The more I watched her and asked questions, the more I liked the idea of cutting out those pieces and putting back them back together like "puzzle pieces." Of course with a lot of encouragement and help from Marie, I set out to work on my first quilt, which turned out to be a Card Tricks quilt.

She didn't have the heart to tell me I was crazy for picking that as my first project.

In 1985, methods such as "strip piecing", "half square triangles" and short-cut methods were still yet to come to quilting. In fact, rotary cutting was just becoming a new trend for quicker cutting, which brings me to the reason for this book…a quicker method to make a Double Wedding Ring quilt.

For years I wanted to make a Double Wedding ring quilt. I tried many different patterns and used all the hints and tips that were out there, to make the quilt; without success. I thought there had to be an easier and faster way to do this. Everyone else had a "short-cut" method to speed up the piecing process, so why not this particular pattern? The traditional way is a tried and true method that will never be obsolete for some people but the curved piecing is just not for me.

I hope you enjoy this Book, find it helpful and inspiring. I wish you much success in making your own Double Wedding ring quilt.

NOTE: Instructions in this Book are for the top of the quilt only. You will have to refer to other sources for finishing your project.

CUTTING INSTRUCTIONS:

Instructions are for an approximate 83-1/2" x 94" quilt top (7 squares across and 8 squares down).

Cut 56 - 11" x 11" squares of the background fabric for the blocks.

Cut 30 - 11" x 5" squares of the background fabric for the 1/2 blocks.

Cut 4 - 5-1/2" x 5-1/2" squares of the background fabric for the corner pieces.

Cut 1016 scrap pieces using the "#1" template piece.

> If using the "All-In-One" piece template, cut 254 pieces.

Cut 254 scrap pieces using the "#2 Left" template (for the left side).

Cut 254 scrap pieces using the "#2 Right" template (for the right side).

> If using the "All-In-One", the "#2 Left and Right" template pieces are already included.

Cut 284 - 3" x 3" pieces using the solid colored fabric.

SUPPLY LIST

- Background Fabric (White on White, Muslin…your choice) (For a king sized quilt, you will need approximately 8 yards of background fabric).
- Solid and patterned fabrics in assorted colors (For the solid and patterned fabric I always use scraps, so I really cannot give you an estimate on fabric here).
- Acrylic Rulers (6" x 12" and 12-1/2" Square Up Ruler)
- Double Wedding Ring Acrylic Templates (A Paper template is available upon request; Email: easydwr@doubleweddingringquilts.com
- Gridded Cutting Mat
- Rotary Cutter with a sharp blade
- Straight pins
- 1/4" measuring tool
- 1/4" Steam-A-Seam2 by The Warm Company(t) (approximately 6 packages).
- Sewing Machine with supply of needles (I use an embroidery needle for the blanket stitch)

- 1/4" foot on your sewing machine (Make sure it is compatible with your sewing machine).
- Thread
- Sharps or Milliner's needles (if preferred method will be appliqué)
- Iron
- Clover Mini Iron (Great for applying the Steam A Seam)

(The supplies above can be found at my Double Wedding Ring Quilts blog; http://doubleweddingringquilts.com/supplies-for-the-easy-dwr-quilt

NOTE: To be compliant with FTC Regulations, I want to inform you that "I may or may not receive compensation when products herein are purchased through the links and site listed in this book."
Thank you, Monna Ellithorpe

STARTING YOUR QUILT…

As with any quilt you make, use the best quality fabrics that you can afford and always make sure to buy enough, should you make a mistake. Of course this is a perfect time for you to use your scraps.

Are you ready to start? That's great, dig in and start cutting and piecing.

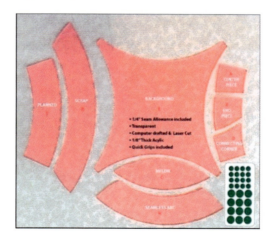

I use the Double Wedding ring acrylic templates pictured on the previous page and all instructions in this book are based on these templates.

CUTTING...

Cut (16) of the "#1" template piece for one block. This will form the arcs. The numbers are marked on the templates when you download them. The "All-In-One" template pictured can be used instead of the (4) "#1" pieces to form the arc.

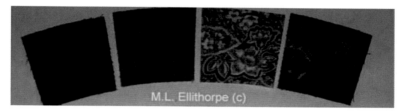

Sew (4) "#1" pieces together to form the arc using a scant 1/4" seam allowance. You will need four arcs per block.

Cut (1) piece each from the "#2 Left and Right" template piece for each end of the arc. Sew a "#2 Left" piece to the left side of the (4) #1 pieces and a "#2 Right" piece to the right side of the (4) #1 pieces and press your seams to one side or open, your choice.

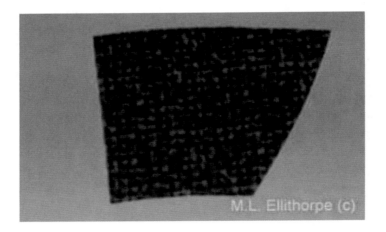

NOTE: Cutting directions are based on the paper template at the end of the book. Template is not to scale. Contact me at: Email: easydwr@doubleweddingringquilts.com

to receive a PDF version of the template.

APPLYING STEAM-A-SEAM2

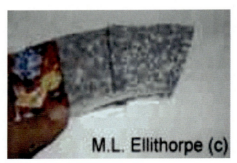

Now that you have many, many arcs made, go to the ironing board with your Steam-A-Seam2.

Begin by laying the un-papered side of the 1/4" tape on the edge of one of the arcs and iron it down, edging your way along until you have secured the Steam-A-Seam2 along the length of your fabric piece.

Do the same on the bottom edge. Complete this on all of the pieces. Let them cool before trying to remove the paper covering.

After they have cooled, remove the paper from the Steam-A-Seam2 on all of the pieces.

Fold the edge of the piece down to form the 1/4" seam and iron in place…do this on all of the pieces.

From here you will need to decide which way you would prefer to complete your blocks. The pieces in their stage right now can be pinned to the background fabric and appliquéd by hand or by machine.

I do not have much luck with pinning, so I use the Steam-A-Seam2 one more time and apply to the edges of the arcs.

The Steam-A-Seam2 will not gum up the needle in your sewing machine.

I have made many of these blocks with this method with no gumming of the needle. After applying the Steam-A-Seam2 again and letting them cool, remove the paper backing and you are now ready to apply the pieces to the background fabric.

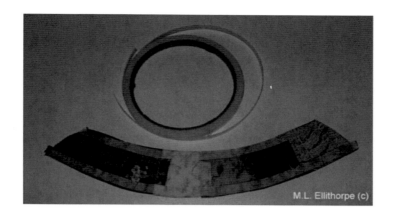

Before cutting your background fabric, iron and starch the fabric (starch is optional).

Cut your background fabric into 11" x 11" squares.

Fold the square in half and finger press about a 1" crease in the fold.

Open and fold in half again the opposite side and finger press a crease in the center.

WORKING WITH THE BACKGROUND

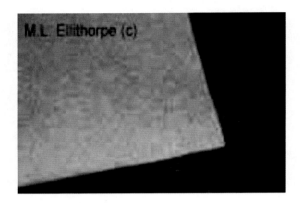

With your background fabric lying flat, take one of the arc pieces and find the center-sewn seam and align it up with the finger pressed fold.

With your 1/4" measuring tool, measure 1/4" from the edge of the arc piece to the edge of the background fabric and finger press the arc down.

The Steam-A-Seam2 will hold temporarily and can be repositioned at this point. Repeat this with all four arc pieces.

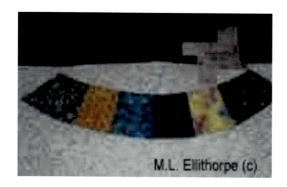

With the arc pieces temporarily secured to the background fabric, making sure they are in position, iron them down permanently and let cool.

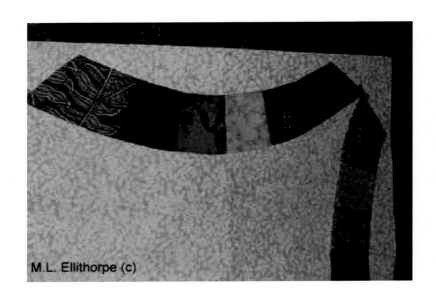

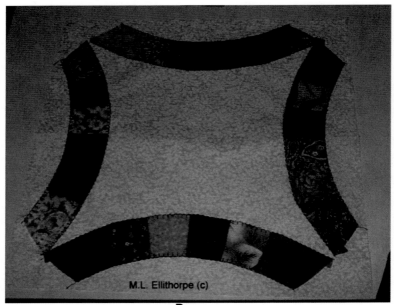

Sew the arc pieces to the background fabric (i.e. appliqué by hand or machine, blanket stitch by hand or machine). I have chosen to secure my arcs with a blanket stitch with my sewing machine.

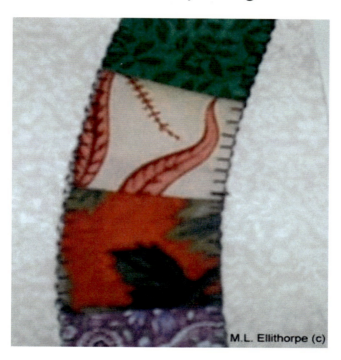

APPLYING CORNER OR

CONNECTING SQUARES

Using your solid colored fabric, cut out (4) blocks measuring 3" x 3" in different colors. Fold in half diagonally and iron a crease in the square.

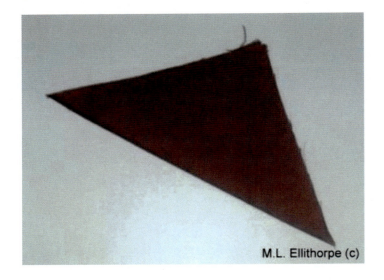

M.L. Ellithorpe (c)

Open the 3" x 3" square up and place the squares on your background fabric at the corners covering the edges of the arcs.

Align the edges of the square with the edge of the background fabric. Do this on all four corners. Sew along the line that you pressed into the 3" x 3" square. Open and press the square toward the outer corner.

On the corners you now have three layers of fabric. You can choose to leave all three in place or trim either the second colored layer or the bottom background layer to about 1/4" from your sewn seam.

If you leave all three layers you will have to deal with greater thickness in the corners when sewing your blocks together.

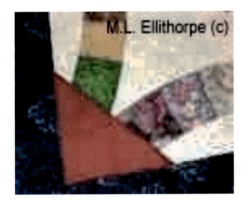

Your individual Double Wedding Ring block is completed and ready to be sewn into rows.

JOINING YOUR QUILT BLOCKS

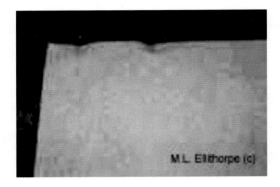

Place two blocks, right sides together, aligning the corner edges and the corner pieces and pin.

Sew together with a scant 1/4" seam. I make it a habit to reverse and sew a couple of extra stitches at the sections where the solid corners pieces meet.

Open and press the seams to one side or open (I press my seams open).

Continue this process until you have the desired quilt size you want.

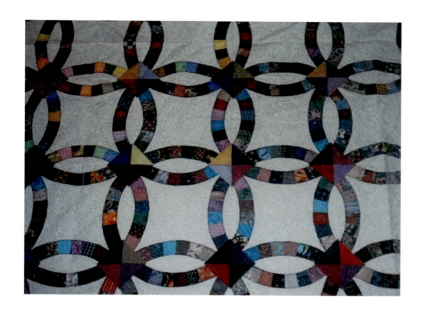

MAKING THE HALF BLOCKS FOR THE QUILT EDGE

From your background fabric, cut pieces measuring 11" x 5-1/2".

These will be your half pieces to finish the ring pattern around the edge of the quilt.

Fold your background piece on the 11" side in half and finger press a crease.

With your background fabric lying flat, take one of the arcs and find the center-sewn seam and align it up with the finger pressed fold.

With your 1/4" measuring tool, measure 1/4" from the edge of the arc to the edge of the background fabric and finger press the arc down.

The Steam-A-Seam2 will hold temporarily and can be repositioned at this point.

Repeat this step, putting only one arc on the background fabric for as many times as needed to go around your quilt.

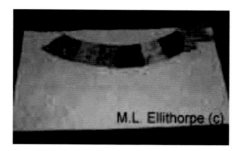

Sew the arcs to the background fabric (i.e. appliqué by hand or machine, blanket stitch by hand or machine).

Again, I have chosen to secure the arcs with a blanket stitch with my sewing machine.

Using your solid colored fabric, cut out (2) blocks measuring 3" x 3" in different colors.

Fold in half and iron a crease in the square.

Open the corner square up and place the squares on your background fabric with the arc.

Align the edges of the square with the edge of the background fabric.

Do this on the two corners. Sew along the line that you pressed into the 3" x 3" square.

Open and press the square toward the outer corner.

Again, on the corners, you have three layers of fabric. You can choose to leave all three in place or trim either the second colored layer or the bottom background layer to about 1/4" from your sewn seam.

Sew the 11" x 5-1/2" pieces end to end. Lay the strip face down on your quilt piece, align the seam lines, corners and corner pieces and sew together with a scant 1/4" seam.

Cut (4) 5-1/2" x 5-1/2" squares out of your background fabric and sew into the corners of your quilt top. This will be the hardest part of the quilt top, as it requires a set in seam.

There are several ways that you can finish the edges. If you like the look of a more traditional Double Wedding Ring quilt, trim around each outer ring making a scalloped edge, put together with backing, batting and bias binding to finish the quilt.

To continue with the easy method, trim the outer edges to 1/2" or 1/4" from the edges of the colored corner pieces, put together with backing, batting and binding to finish the quilt.

Remember to sew a label to the back of your quilt with your signature, the date and who you are presenting the quilt to with your city and state.

I hope you found these instructions easy to follow. If you have any questions, please do not hesitate to contact me.
easydwr@doubleweddingringquilts.com

TEMPLATES

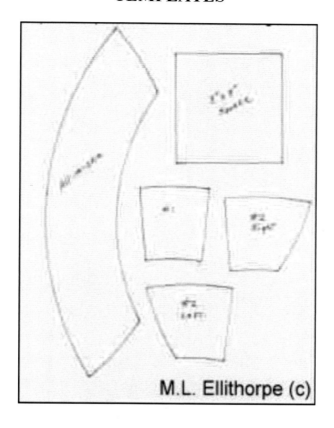

All Rights Reserved © Easy Double Wedding Ring Quilt Pattern - 2nd Edition - Monna Ellithorpe 2004 – 2015

NOTE: Every effort has been made to ensure the accuracy of the templates when printed but because of the variations in printers on the market, the templates may not print accurately.

About The Author - Monna Ellithorpe

Where to Find Monna Ellithorpe Online

Website: http://doubleweddingringquilts.com
http://monnaellithorpe.com/

Twitter: http://twitter.com/dwrquilts
http://twitter.com/msellithorpe

Facebook:
https://www.facebook.com/monna.ellithorpe.1
https://www.facebook.com/BlueJeanWriter.MonnaEllithorpe

LinkedIn: https://www.linkedin.com/in/monnaellithorpe

Amazon Author Page:
http://www.amazon.com/-/e/B0078G3JZ2

Google +
https://plus.google.com/u/0/b/10451713554371783
1383/+Doubleweddingringquilts

https://plus.google.com/u/0/+MonnaEllithorpe

THE END

Made in the USA
Las Vegas, NV
04 April 2024